The Great Civil War Draft Riots

CORNERSTONES
OF FREEDOM™

SECOND SERIES

Deborah Kent

Children's Press®
A Division of Scholastic Inc.
New York • Toronto • London • Auckland • Sydney
Mexico City • New Delhi • Hong Kong
Danbury, Connecticut

Photographs © 2005: Art Resource, NY/HIP/Scala: 3; Boston Public
Library: 30; Brown Brothers: 16; Corbis Images: 5, 6, 13, 18, 25, 28,
29, 34, 40 (Bettmann), 20 (Leonard de Selva), 9 (Medford Historical
Society Collection), 14 (Charles G. Rosenberg/Museum of the City of
New York), cover, 8, 15, 21, 22, 24, 31, 35, 41, 44 top right, 45 bottom
right; Getty Images/Hulton Archive: 7, 44 left (Johnson Wilson & Co.),
38; Library of Congress: 10, 11, 19, 26, 36, 44 bottom, 45 top left;
New-York Historical Society: 32; Stock Montage, Inc.: 4, 12, 27.

Library of Congress Cataloging-in-Publication Data
Kent, Deborah.
  The great Civil War draft riots / Deborah Kent. — 1st ed.
       p. cm. — (Cornerstones of freedom)
  Includes bibliographical references and index.
  ISBN 0-516-23632-6
  1. Draft Riot, New York, N.Y., 1863—Juvenile literature. 2. New York
(N.Y.)—History—Civil War, 1861–1865—Juvenile literature. I. Title.
II. Series.
  F128.44.K46 2005
  974.7'103—dc22   2004014454

CHILDREN'S PRESS, and CORNERSTONES OF FREEDOM™, and
associated logos are trademarks and/or registered trademarks of
Scholastic Library Publishing. SCHOLASTIC and associated logos
are trademarks and/or registered trademarks of Scholastic Inc.

1 2 3 4 5 6 7 8 9 10 R 14 13 12 11 10 09 08 07 06 05

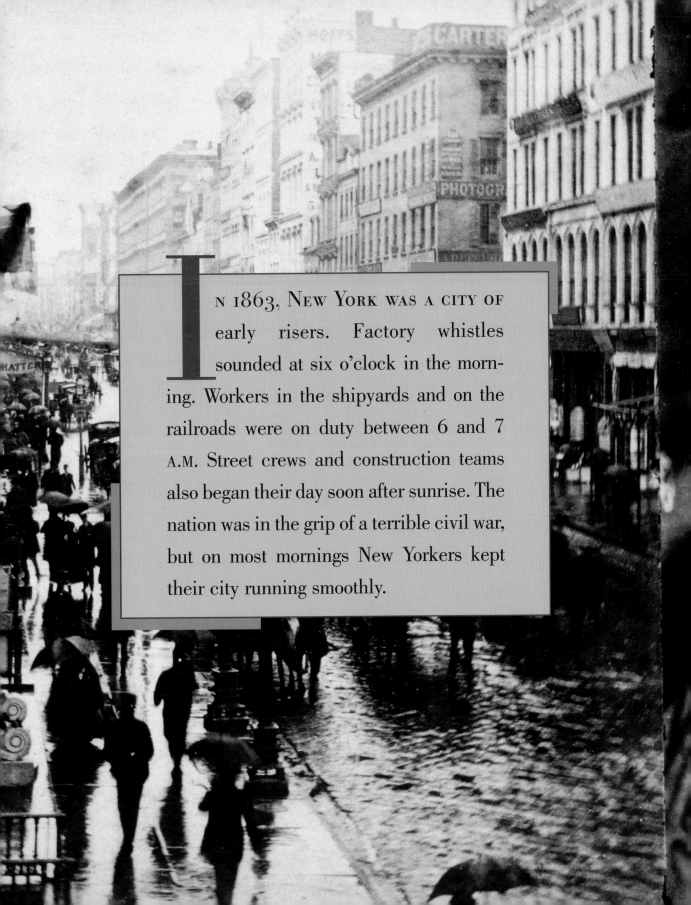

IN 1863, NEW YORK WAS A CITY OF early risers. Factory whistles sounded at six o'clock in the morning. Workers in the shipyards and on the railroads were on duty between 6 and 7 A.M. Street crews and construction teams also began their day soon after sunrise. The nation was in the grip of a terrible civil war, but on most mornings New Yorkers kept their city running smoothly.

Hundreds of protestors march to the provost marshal's office in New York City to protest the scheduled draft lottery.

On the morning of July 13, however, hundreds of New Yorkers failed to appear on the job. Instead, they came together in the streets and formed ragged columns. Slowly, they marched toward the office of the Ninth District Provost Marshal at Third Avenue and Forty-sixth Street. Many of the marchers wore signs with the words: **NO DRAFT!** They planned to protest the draft lottery to be held at the provost marshal's office that day. The lottery was a means of choosing names by chance to determine which men would have to serve in the army.

Along the way, some of the marchers broke into a hardware store. They grabbed several axes, which they used to chop down telegraph poles. Other protesters, including a band of women, tore up railroad tracks and stopped train service along Second and Third avenues.

Policemen rushed to the scene and tried to stop the violence. The crowd attacked them, throwing bricks and

The Ninth District Provost Marshal's office burns on July 13, 1863. Draft protestors set the building on fire as the draft lottery was taking place.

cobblestones. Police superintendent John A. Kennedy was seized, beaten, and dragged through the mud.

As the crowd milled outside, the draft selection process got under way. Officials spun a wheel that released names at random. Each man whose name was selected would be required to serve in the Union army.

More than fifty names had been drawn when a pistol shot rang out. On this signal, a band of firemen rushed into the draft office. The firemen smashed the selection wheel and set the building on fire. The episode known to historians as the New York City Draft Riots had begun in earnest.

★ ★ ★ ★

In the early 1800s, the economy of the Southern states relied heavily on the use of slaves, such as these black men and women picking cotton on a plantation.

NORTH VS. SOUTH

In the early 1800s, life in the Northern United States was very different from life in the South. Farming was important in both regions, but the North was turning more and more toward manufacturing. Northern factories churned out textiles and other goods. The South had few factories and relied almost entirely on farming. The Southern economy depended largely on cotton. Owners of cotton **plantations** counted on slaves to plant, tend, and harvest their crops.

Slavery had existed in the United States since its beginnings. By the 1850s, however, most Northern states had outlawed the practice. Slavery was still practiced throughout the South.

When Abraham Lincoln was elected president of the United States in 1860, many Southerners were horrified. They believed that Lincoln would try to put an end to slavery. Before he was elected, Lincoln had said that he wanted to keep slavery from spreading into new states and territories. He had promised not to end slavery in states where it already existed.

Abraham Lincoln was born on February 12, 1809, in Kentucky. He served as 16th president of the United States from 1861 to 1865.

Fort Sumter is located in Charleston, South Carolina, at the entrance to the city's harbor. In 1948, the Fort Sumter National Monument was established to preserve the fort's history as the site of the first battle of the Civil War (1861–1865).

Many Southerners doubted that Lincoln would keep this promise. They were outraged by the idea that the federal government in Washington, D.C., might force the South to give up slavery and destroy their way of life.

Shortly after Lincoln's election, South Carolina **seceded,** or left the United States. Ten more Southern states seceded in 1861. Hoping to preserve the Southern way of life, they formed their own nation called the Confederate States of America. On April 12, 1861, Confederate cannons fired on

Union troops stationed at Fort Sumter, South Carolina. Those first shots marked the beginning of the bloody conflict known as the American Civil War.

In the early days of the war, volunteers rushed to join the army in both the North and the South. Most were farm boys eager for adventure. All were ready to fight for their country. No one expected the war to last more than a few months, and the boys didn't want to miss the excitement. By August 1861, the Union army had swelled to about 500,000 men. About 350,000 men had **enlisted** in the South.

THE BATTLE OF BULL RUN

On July 21, 1861, hundreds of people gathered in Manassas, Virginia. It was the site of the first Civil War battle, and no one wanted to miss it. Ladies came in their gowns and bonnets, and children played games and ate picnic lunches. But the First Battle of Bull Run, as it came to be called, was no picnic. When the fighting was over, nearly 3,000 Union troops and 2,000 Confederates were dead, wounded, captured, or missing. It became all too clear that the war would be more costly than anyone had ever dreamed.

Union officers pose outside a tent. In the early years of the war, men in the North and the South rushed to volunteer to fight for their cause.

A blindfolded man draws names of those who will be required to enlist. After the National Conscription Act was passed, draft lotteries were held to determine who would serve in the Union army.

Tragically, the war was not over in a few short months. The lists of dead and wounded on both sides grew longer day by day. Property was destroyed, and families were overcome with grief. Both North and South grew weary of the struggle. By 1863, the Union army was at dangerously low numbers. Fewer and fewer men wanted to volunteer for military service. The army desperately needed fresh **recruits.**

THE PRICE OF WAR

To fill the ranks, President Lincoln signed the National **Conscription** Act in March 1863. The act allowed the federal government to draft men into the army. A certain number of men from each state would be selected and required to serve. Federal provost marshals were assigned to different parts of the Union. These officials were ordered to hold lotteries that randomly selected the names of men to be drafted into the army.

10

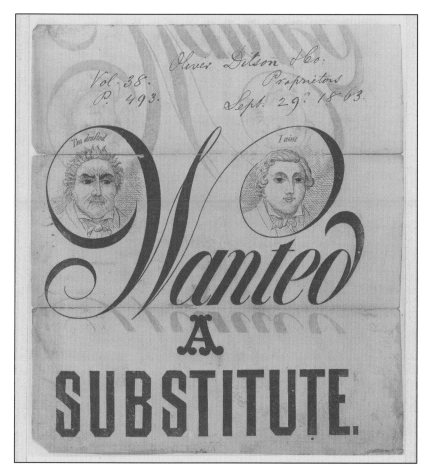

A poster advertises a man's desire to find a substitute to take his place in the army. Those who were wealthy enough could pay three hundred dollars to avoid the draft, others could avoid serving if they found someone willing to take their place.

Many Americans found the draft law deeply disturbing. It meant that, against their will, thousands of young men would be taken away from their families and their work. By order of the government, these men would be sent to risk their lives on the battlefields.

Not every man who was ordered to serve would actually have to go to war, however. The law stated that a man could avoid the draft if he paid three hundred dollars, or he could find another man willing to fight in his place.

Many people living in northern cities in the 1800s were poor immigrants who complained that the draft was unfair. These poor people could not afford to pay three hundred dollars to avoid serving in the army.

In 1863, three hundred dollars was a large sum of money. A laborer might hope to earn that much in one year. Only the rich could easily afford to pay this amount.

Many people thought that this way of avoiding the draft was not fair to the poor. Even the *New York Daily News* wrote about the unfairness of the law. "The fact that the Conscription virtually exempts the rich and fastens its iron hand upon the poor alone is sufficient demonstration of its injustice." Protests against the Conscription Act broke out in cities all over the North.

The most powerful antidraft movement of all sprang up in New York City. New York was the nation's biggest city and its financial capital. In 1863, New York City consisted only of the island of Manhattan. (The other boroughs that are part of New York City today—Brooklyn, Queens, Staten Island, and the Bronx—were not added until the 1890s.)

During the Civil War, most New Yorkers were crowded into the southern (lower) end of Manhattan. Upper Manhattan was still largely rural. Manufacturing, shipping, and banking were the city's major industries. Wealthy New Yorkers tended to live near the center of the island. Poorer people, both white and black, clustered along the waterfronts formed by the East and Hudson rivers.

Dirty, crowded tenement buildings were home to many of New York City's poor immigrants in the 1860s.

A BUBBLING STEW

New York City has sometimes been described as a vast melting pot. It is a place where people from different backgrounds blend together. In the 1860s, however, the city was like a stew whose ingredients had scarcely begun to blend.

The wealthiest and most powerful people in the city were white Protestants of English and Dutch origin. Many of

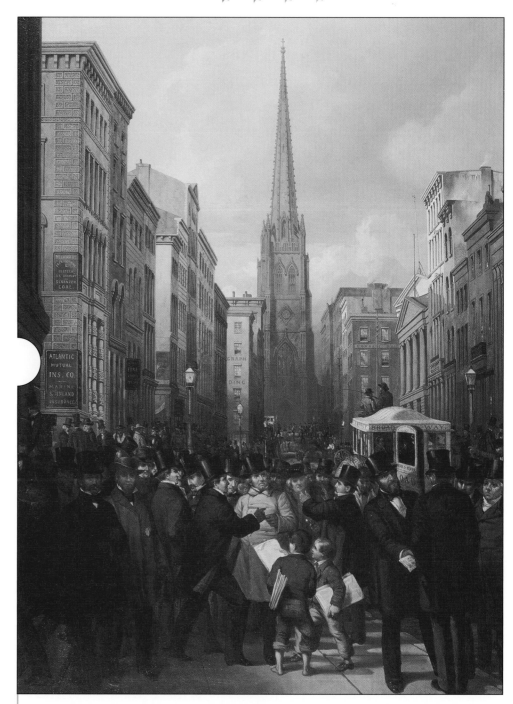

Wall Street was already the financial capital of the United States when the Civil War started. The offices of the many businesses owned by wealthy New Yorkers were located there.

Craftsmen work at forging iron in a factory in New York City in the 1800s.

these New Yorkers were the descendants of settlers who arrived in the 1600s and 1700s. For the most part, they controlled the city's government and finances.

Another group consisted of recent immigrants from Germany. Most of the Germans were also Protestants. They tended to work in skilled trades. They were carpenters, blacksmiths, stonecutters, and shipbuilders.

The third major group in New York at the time of the Civil War consisted of African Americans. Most of these people were free blacks who had lived in the city for generations.

The neighborhood known as Five Points was New York City's most notorious slum in the 1800s. Home to many immigrants from Ireland, it was a dangerous place to live.

Until the 1840s, African Americans traditionally held the lowest-paying jobs in the city. Black men worked as bricklayers, whitewashers, longshoremen (dockworkers), barbers, and restaurant waiters. Black women often held positions as household servants—cooking, sewing, and washing clothes.

*　*　*　*

During the 1840s and 1850s, thousands of Irish Catholics poured into New York City. The Irish came to the United States when a disastrous famine, or food shortage, swept their homeland. Most of the Irish people who made their way to New York were uneducated and very poor. They were grateful to take any jobs they could find.

When the Irish immigrants arrived, they competed with African Americans for many of the same jobs. The Irish were willing to work for even lower wages than were the blacks. As a result, they took over many of the jobs that blacks had filled. Sometimes Irish workers went on **strike** to demand better pay and safer working conditions. Employers brought in African Americans to break the strikes—that is, to work when the strikers walked off the job. Tension mounted even more between the African Americans and the Irish.

THE FIVE POINTS

The Irish immigrants who flocked to New York hoped to build a better life. Often those hopes were crushed all too quickly. Life for the Irish in New York was filled with toil and terrible poverty. One of the poorest Irish neighborhoods was a section of Lower Manhattan known as the Five Points. After a visit to the city in the 1840s, English novelist Charles Dickens described the Five Points neighborhood: "These narrow ways . . . [reek] everywhere with dirt and filth. . . . All that is loathsome, drooping, and decayed is here."

Making matters worse, many white New Yorkers had **racist** attitudes toward blacks. Whites generally believed that African Americans were an **inferior** race. Because they looked down on African Americans, whites resented any gains they made.

White laborers were deeply concerned over the Conscription Act. They feared that conscription would weigh most heavily on them. Slaves and freedmen (former slaves) were

The Irish Emigrant Aid
society was established
in 1841 to protect the
interests of the thousands
of Irish immigrants who
settled in New York City.

not considered citizens, so they could not be drafted. Irish and German workers would be sent off to war while former slaves stayed in New York to take their jobs. At the same time, the wealthy could buy their way out of the draft. The Conscription Act seemed to favor rich whites and poor blacks, while targeting white wage earners.

New York City also faced serious divisions in politics. Both Republicans and Democrats had a strong presence on New York's political scene. In general, Republicans opposed slavery. They supported President Lincoln and the war.

The Democrats were divided into two camps. The War Democrats were one group. They supported the war because they did not want the

FREE AT LAST!

On January 1, 1863, President Lincoln signed a document called the Emancipation Proclamation. It granted freedom to all slaves living in the Southern states that had seceded. The Confederacy, however, did not recognize laws made by the U.S. government, so the proclamation could not be enforced, or put into effect. Still, this document was important. It showed slaves that the president of the United States would uphold their right to freedom. If the Union won the war, slavery would come to an end.

After the Battle of Antietem in September 1862, Lincoln told the Southern states that they had until 1863 to pledge their allegiance to the Union. If they didn't, he would declare that their slaves were free. None of the Southern states returned to the Union and Lincoln followed through by issuing the Emancipation Proclamation on January 1, 1863.

Black slaves were considered property and sold at auctions to the highest bidders.

South to secede from the Union. However, they did not take a strong stand against slavery. The Peace Democrats, or Copperheads, opposed the war. They argued that the Southern states should be allowed to secede if they chose to do so.

The National Conscription Act sparked heated debate among these groups. Republicans favored the draft, while Democrats opposed it. The War Democrats hoped that the courts would stop the draft. Copperheads said that the people should take matters into their own hands. They felt that the people should resist an unjust law that would only prolong the war.

A political cartoon from the Civil War era shows Copperheads, or Peace Democrats, as a threat to the Union because of their opposition to the war.

★ ★ ★ ★

TERROR IN THE STREETS

On Saturday, July 11, 1863, the first draft lottery in New York City got under way. The lottery wheels released the names of 1,236 young men. Each would be called on for military service. Most of these men would be released from military duty because of health problems or the needs of their families. But some would be forced to go to war.

The names of the men who will be forced to serve in the Union army are chosen during a draft lottery. Some of those chosen were excused from duty because of health problems or the needs of their families.

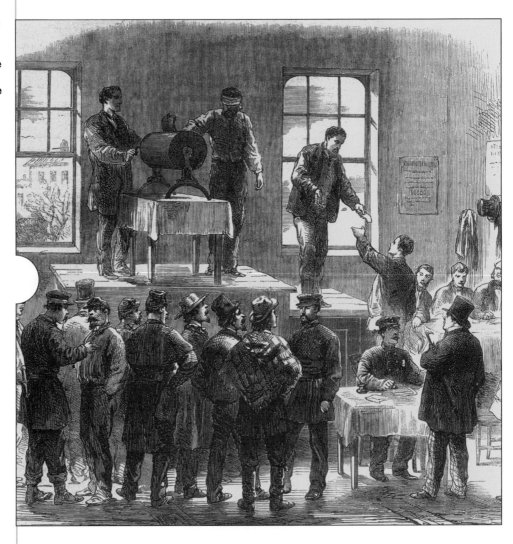

* * * *

The morning after the first draft lottery, New York newspapers printed the list of names that had been drawn. At the same time, the papers printed the long list of deaths from the Battle of Gettysburg. This battle had been fought in Pennsylvania less than two weeks before. Some 23,000 Union soldiers had died or been wounded at Gettysburg. Now the government was ordering more men to prepare for the same fate.

In neighborhoods throughout the city, people gathered to talk and plan. Leaders were chosen and groups were formed. By Monday morning, thousands of people were ready to stop the draft process by violent means. The first step was the attack on the provost marshal's office at Third Avenue and Forty-sixth Street.

As the provost marshal's office burned, officials ordered that the draft be stopped. The rioters hardly seemed to notice or care. Instead, the riot gained strength. The columns of protesters became a raging mob. Many people forgot the original purpose, which was to stop the draft. They simply let loose their anger at those who they believed were responsible for the war.

More and more people poured into the streets. Some were simply curious. Excited by the noise and the taste of danger, some joined the protesters. To gather still more people, the protesters burst into factories and forced the workers to join them. By the afternoon, business in the city was at a

THE BATTLE OF GETTYSBURG

From July 1 through July 3, 1863, Union and Confederate forces clashed at the town of Gettysburg, Pennsylvania. Both sides suffered terrible losses. Some 50,000 men were killed or wounded. Gettysburg was the bloodiest battle ever fought on the North American continent. The following November, Abraham Lincoln visited the battlefield. It was then that he delivered his famous Gettysburg Address.

Although officials ordered the lottery stopped when the provost marshal's office was burned, protestors continued rioting. They burned other draft offices and attacked police officers who tried to stop them.

The draft protestors turned into an angry mob that destroyed property and stole anything that could be carried away.

standstill. As one reporter explained, "Men left their various pursuits; owners of stores put up their shutters; factories were emptied, conductors or drivers left their [streetcars]."

Bands of rioters burned other draft offices. They attacked policemen who tried to stop them. They broke into wealthy homes on fashionable Lexington Avenue and stole anything they could carry away: jewelry, picture frames, clocks, china, and even furniture.

Some turned their fury upon the office of the *New York Tribune*. Horace Greeley, the *Tribune*'s editor, was a dedi-

A VOICE FOR ABOLITION

Horace Greeley was a strong voice in favor of the abolition of slavery. In 1841, he founded the *New York Tribune,* a daily newspaper that served the Northern states. Before the Civil War, the *Tribune* opposed the spread of slavery into the Western states. Greeley praised President Lincoln for signing the Emancipation Proclamation, which roused the anger of many Democrats in New York.

cated **abolitionist.** He believed that slavery should come to an end. Rioters tried to set the *Tribune* building on fire, but the police managed to drive them away.

A TURN FOR THE WORSE

By Monday afternoon, the riots took an ugly turn. The rioters directed their rage against the city's African Americans. Small boys roamed the streets, tossing stones at the windows of buildings where black people lived. Later, older boys and grown men looted and burned these "marked" houses.

Horace Greeley was born in Amherst, New Hampshire, on February 3, 1811. He founded the *New York Tribune* in 1841 and served as its editor until his death in 1872.

26

African Americans were targeted by the draft protestors because they were not citizens and couldn't be drafted into the Union army. The protestors' rage led them to attack, and in some cases kill, black men.

On the streets, black men were attacked at random. One crowd of rioters set upon William Jones. Jones was a black man walking home from a bakery with a loaf of bread. The mob beat him unconscious and hanged him from a lamppost.

Another mob of some four hundred rioters attacked an orphanage for black children. While the rioters were breaking down the front door, the staff managed to lead all 237 children out a rear exit and get them to safety. The mob tore through the beautiful old building and burned it

New York's Sullivan Street was home to many blacks at the time of the draft riots.

to the ground. They even chopped down the surrounding shade trees.

The violence increased over the days that followed. Blacks—particularly black men—remained prime targets. Some white laborers seemed determined to force black workers out of the city.

Members of the Longshoremen's Association, an organization of white dockworkers, guarded the piers. According to the *New York Daily News*, the longshoremen "insisted that the colored people must and shall be driven to other departments of industry, and that the work upon the docks . . . shall be attended to solely and absolutely by members of the Longshoremen's Association, and such white laborers as they see fit to permit upon the premises."

Republicans and figures of authority were also attacked. Rioters seized and battered dozens of draft officials, soldiers, and police. Women took an active role in this kind of rioting. One eyewitness wrote, "[Women] vow **vengeance**

Rioters attacked African
American men, women, and
children. Many black families locked themselves in
their homes while others
fled the city in an attempt
to escape the violence.

on all enrolling officers and provost marshals and regret
that they did not annihilate [destroy] the officers when they
first called to procure the names for the draft."

The riots spread terror over the city. Fearing for their
lives, most African Americans hid behind locked doors.
Others fled to Long Island and New Jersey. Whites who had
supported the antislavery movement also tried to stay out
of sight. Mattie Griffith, an active abolitionist, watched the

Mattie Griffith was an abolitionist who wrote the book *Autobiography of a Slave*. She was born in Kentucky and, because of an inheritance, became the owner of several slaves. After her book was published, the American Anti-Slavery Society gave her the money that allowed her to return to Kentucky to free and resettle her slaves.

* * * *

riot from her apartment window. In a letter to a friend, she described "the strange wretched abandoned creatures that flocked out from their dens and lairs." The nightmarish chaos in the city left her with "a confused sense of half-being."

THE BATTLE FOR CONTROL

When the draft riots erupted on July 13, New York was ill-equipped to restore order. The state **militia** was busy chasing General Robert E. Lee's forces in Pennsylvania. A handful of troops defended New York at the Navy Yard and several small forts. The Metropolitan Police Force was the main body available to control the rioters.

It was up to New York City mayor George Opdyke and New York State governor Horatio Seymour to end the riots. At first, the mayor tried to strengthen the city's police force. He urged loyal citizens to report to police headquarters. There they would be given assignments as emergency deputies.

★ ★ ★ ★

Police officers work to stop
the draft riots. The mayor of
New York City called upon
citizens to report to police
headquarters and become
emergency deputies to help
calm the riots.

Hundreds of New Yorkers responded to the call. Many
New Yorkers who had been involved in the demonstrations
that morning were there. These demonstrators had only
meant to protest the draft. Now, they were troubled by the
rising violence. Among those who worked to restore order
were hundreds of New York City firefighters. Firemen had
burned the provost marshal's office on Monday morning, but

for the next three days they struggled bravely to protect lives and property.

Word of the unrest soon reached the governor's mansion in Albany. Governor Seymour rushed to New York City. Seymour was a Democrat and was not in favor of the draft law. In the city, he gave speeches in an effort to calm the protesters. The governor admitted that the draft was unjust and that the rioters had a right to be upset. But he also stressed the need for peaceful negotiations, or talks, between protesters and the authorities.

Horatio Seymour was governor of New York from 1863 to 1865. He was the Democratic candidate for president in 1868, but lost the election to Ulysses S. Grant.

By Tuesday morning, the rioters fought for control of the streets. With furniture and scrap lumber, they set up barricades, or fences, along some of the city's major avenues. This made it difficult for the police to arrest the rioters and restore order. The rioters also tried to take over factories that produced firearms. Brutal clashes between rioters and police occurred at firearms plants such as the Union Steam Works on East Twenty-second Street. Police and rioters fought hand to hand with clubs, knives, and axes, up and down stairways and across factory floors.

The New York Draft Riots lasted for four days.

At times, bands of rioters searched from house to house. They dragged out soldiers and policemen and beat them without mercy. The police and the military also conducted house searches, looking for rioters and weapons. In the riot-torn neighborhoods, no one felt safe. All was noise, bloodshed, and fear.

The rioters refused to negotiate with city officials. It was clear that more help was needed. On Tuesday, Mayor Opdyke contacted Washington and asked for more federal troops.

The troops marched into the city on Wednesday, July 15. Their mission was to restore order, but at first the soldiers caused still greater bloodshed. They tore down barricades and fired bullets into crowds of rioters. In fact, the most deaths occurred as a result of clashes between the soldiers and the mobs. The sheer number of troops, combined with their superior organization and weapons, finally brought the riots to an end on Thursday.

New Yorkers were deeply shaken. Hundreds of homes, factories, and office buildings were in ruins. Property damage was thought to be around $1.5 million. At least 119 men, women, and children were dead. How could the city recover from such a disaster?

REBUILDING AND REFLECTING

On Friday, July 17, New York's archbishop John Hughes spoke to a crowd of five thousand people. Most of them were Irish Catholics. Among the city's Catholics, Hughes was deeply respected and loved. The archbishop was ill and

By the time the draft riots were over, property damage in New York City totaled nearly $1,500,000.

weak, and this was his last public appearance. He told the people that they must bear their hurts and disappointments with patience. He cautioned them against the use of violence. He also urged them to seek change by exercising their right to vote. Archbishop Hughes' speech was an important first step toward healing in the riot-torn city.

John Hughes was born in Ireland in 1797. He immigrated to the United States in 1816 and was ordained a priest in 1826. Appointed archbishop of New York in 1850, he helped bring the draft riots to an end.

Government officials and citizens across the Union had watched anxiously during the riots. If New York successfully rejected the draft, other cities would surely follow. The Union army would be weakened as a result. If they thought the Union cause was floundering, Great Britain, France, and other European nations might enter the war on the side of the Confederacy. Thus the outcome of the war could depend on the way problems in New York were resolved.

Some Republicans wanted Lincoln to place New York City under **martial** law. This meant that the military would take complete control over the city and maintain order by force. Lincoln believed that martial law would incite New Yorkers to further violence. Instead, Mayor Opdyke and Governor Seymour remained in charge. Lincoln appointed General John A. Dix to head the Department of the East, the military division that defended the New York area.

Governor Seymour continued to hope that the draft would not be enforced. In the weeks after the riots, he sent representatives to Washington to discuss the matter with President Lincoln. Lincoln held firm. He insisted that the draft must go forward in New York and throughout the Union. On August 6, Governor Seymour wrote to a friend that his efforts had been wasted. "I look for nothing but hostility," he added, "but I shall do my duty, demand my rights, and let consequences take care of themselves."

On August 19, the draft lottery reopened in New York City. It was barely a month after the rioting ended. Instead of starting in a working-class district, the draft began in the wealthy Greenwich Village section. Most people in Greenwich Village were Republicans who supported the war. In

* * * *

case of trouble, some 10,000 federal troops were posted around the city. "Everything was as quiet and orderly as a New England sabbath," one soldier wrote. "No disturbance occurred anywhere."

TAMMANY HALL

Tammany Hall began as a secret society in New York City in the late 1700s. In the early 1800s, the Tammany Society formed close ties with the Democratic Party. During and after the Civil War, it controlled large funds to help the poor. Over time, Tammany Hall, as it came to be known, helped many needy people and gained power within the city. But it also misused its power to sway voters and bribe public officials. Its leaders dominated New York City politics until the 1930s.

Before conscription began again, Democratic leaders in New York tried to ease the burden of the draft on the poor. To do this, they sold bonds to raise money. This money could be used to hire substitutes for draftees who did not wish to serve. Firemen, policemen, and men with families to support could get help under this program. The Democrats who organized this fund belonged to a group known as Tammany Hall.

LOOKING TO THE FUTURE

For months after the riots, New York officials gathered reports about the loss of life and property. Money was collected to help families cope with their losses. By most accounts, African American families were given far less money than were white families. Many African Americans left the city after the riots. The black population fell by more than 20 percent. Black people did not return to New York in large numbers until the twentieth century.

One group that made suggestions about preventing future riots was the Association for Improving the Condition of the Poor (AICP). The AICP made a strong case for better

★ ★ ★ ★

Tammany Hall was the headquarters of the organization that exerted great control over New York City's government in the 1800s and early 1900s.

health, education, and housing in the city's poor neighborhoods. One AICP report stated that under better living conditions, people would become so law-abiding "that future riots would be impossible."

After the draft riots of 1863, wealthy New Yorkers took steps to ease the plight of the poor. The city opened medical

Children attend kindergarten in New York in the late 1800s. After the draft riots, officials worked to be sure that more children attended school.

clinics in poor neighborhoods. It passed laws requiring better housing conditions. Officials worked to ensure that all children attended school.

On March 5, 1864, a crowd of some 100,000 people gathered in New York's Union Square. The crowd had assembled to watch the ceremonial presentation of flags to a new regiment of Union army recruits. All of the recruits were African Americans.

The Twentieth New York Regiment was the first regiment of African American volunteers to march out of New York

City. One eyewitness wrote to a friend describing "[the] historic and, to me, great symbolic fact of the presentation of colors to the regiment of blacks in Union Square. There were drawn up in a line over a thousand armed Negroes, where but yesterday they were literally hunted down like rats." Bands played, and the crowd cheered wildly. Straight and proud, the young black troops marched down Broadway to join the fight for freedom.

BLACK REGIMENTS

During the early years of the Civil War, the Union army did not want to enlist African Americans. Military leaders thought that blacks were inferior to whites and would make poor soldiers. The army's policy changed when the Bureau of Colored Troops was established in May 1863. About 200,000 black troops served in the Union army. More than half were former slaves.

The 20th U.S. Colored Infantry Regiment receives its colors on March 5, 1864.

Glossary

abolitionist—person who believed that slavery should come to an end

conscription—military draft

draft—a call to military service

enlist—join the military

inferior—of lower rank or quality

martial—military

militia—a military force that is made up of local citizens, not part of the regular army

plantation—an estate where a large amount of crops are grown

racist—a person who believes that one race is superior to others

recruit—new, recently enlisted soldier

secede—break away from

strike—a group's refusal to work in protest of bad working conditions

vengeance—the act of revenge, or paying back a misdeed

Timeline: The Great

1860

Abraham Lincoln is elected president of the United States; South Carolina secedes from the Union.

1861

Ten more Southern states secede from the Union to form the Confederate States of America; Confederate troops fire on Union forces at Fort Sumter, South Carolina, starting the Civil War.

1863

JANUARY 1
President Lincoln signs the Emancipation Proclamation, freeing the slaves in the Southern states.

MARCH 3
Lincoln signs the National Conscription Act, beginning the military draft.

JULY 11
New York City begins the draft lottery.

JULY 13
Demonstrators interrupt the draft lottery in New York City and spread violence through the city.